Project Dictator
Or 'Why Democracy is Overrated and I Don't Miss It At All'

Rhum + Clay
with Hamish MacDougall

methuen | drama

LONDON • NEW YORK • OXFORD • NEW DELHI • SYDNEY

METHUEN DRAMA
Bloomsbury Publishing Plc
50 Bedford Square, London, WC1B 3DP, UK
1385 Broadway, New York, NY 10018, USA
29 Earlsfort Terrace, Dublin 2, Ireland

BLOOMSBURY, METHUEN DRAMA and the Methuen
Drama logo are trademarks of Bloomsbury Publishing Plc

First published in Great Britain 2023

A catalogue record for this book is available from the British Library.

Library of Congress Control Number: 2023945688

ISBN: PB: 978-1-3504-5178-0
ePDF: 978-1-3504-5179-7
eBook: 978-1-3504-5180-3

Series: Modern Plays

Typeset by Mark Heslington Ltd, Scarborough, North Yorkshire

To find out more about our authors and books visit
www.bloomsbury.com and sign up for our newsletters.

PROJECT DICTATOR

(or 'Why Democracy is Overrated
and I Don't Miss It At All')

A new play by Hamish MacDougall,
Julian Spooner and Matthew Wells

Preface from the writers

Hamish MacDougall on the development of the idea

As with most devised projects, *Project Dictator* started with a simple idea of creating a clowning show about authoritarian politics. It felt right for a couple of reasons; firstly, authoritarian populists were (and sadly still are) on the rise all over the world and it felt right to respond to this. Secondly, there is of course a rich history of clowning speaking to global issues, perhaps the most famous example being Charlie Chaplin's *The Great Dictator*, a satire of Nazism made during World War Two.

The initial idea was to stage a show about two writers who are commissioned to write a play celebrating a dictator's birthday. As we approached our first research and development period this started to not feel right. As a company we questioned who were we as free artists in the UK to make this show. It felt like we were imposing an idea on a subject we only knew through books and articles. This is when we decided that we needed to educate ourselves by talking to artists who had worked under oppression, get their insight and first-hand experience and ultimately make a show that would honour the stories that they told us.

We started creating a call out. Matt and Julian contacted artists they had met in their past international touring. I sought the help of two amazing people connected to my MA at Goldsmiths, one being my professor, Bernadette Buckley, and the other my friend and fellow student, David Labi. Eventually around fifteen artists agreed to speak to us and share their time. It is worth noting here that we promised to keep all the artists anonymous as some still live under oppression, and those who live elsewhere still have family back home and there are security issues about speaking on this subject.

The stories these artists shared were enlightening, humbling and deeply moving. They ranged from stories about oppression starting from school and onwards, imprisonment and torture for the simple act of saying what you think, death threats due to artistic creation and also hope in the future and what that might look like. We told every artist what the idea for the show was and we gained invaluable feedback on the path we should take. It was also encouraging that every artist loved the idea of using humour around this subject, a key theme seemed to be that these regimes despise laughter against them, and humour is a powerful weapon.

After the interviews we had a deep conversation about what path the show should take. The strongest thought to come out of the conversations was that we were sitting in a rehearsal space in London where we could creatively attempt anything we wanted to. What our interviewees had been describing were spaces with no freedom, rooms where you have to watch what you say; in essence a room that controls you. This sparked the idea of creating a show with two distinct halves. One that reflected both realities.

Coincidentally, as we went into rehearsals for the show, Vladimir Putin began his horrific war in Ukraine. As stories started to come out of Russia about artists being censored, imprisoned or escaping, it further brought home to us the reality of the subject we were engaging with. Augusto Boal wrote in *Theatre of the Oppressed* that 'Theatre is a weapon. A very efficient weapon. For this reason, one must fight for it'. We hope that this show adds something, even if it is small, to highlight the struggle of so many artists working around the world today. Without these interviews we would not have made this show and we dedicate the work to our interviewees and all the global artists working to defeat suppression.

Julian Spooner on clowning, populism and politics

During the making of every single Rhum + Clay production we've always kept on asking the same question until we crack it: what's the relationship between the form and the content? What is the relationship between clowning and dictators? Why is this a theatre show and not another form? Initially, we played with the larger-than-life images of dictators themselves; after all, they are often clown- or buffoon-like characters themselves, grotesque in their iconography and imitable ability to lack both self-reflection and self-awareness. We tried a few ideas but were struggling to find anything that excited us; it's like we'd seen it all before. Then we looked at ourselves. As performers and collaborators, Matthew and I had been making work as Rhum + Clay for over a decade and now we were on stage together; just us and a musician. There was a lifetime of material and dynamic to mine through. Hamish, our co-director, began asking us questions about ourselves as performers and clowns: who normally plays the naïve? Who is the boss clown? Who is the disrupter, who wants to keep order? Suddenly, roles started to emerge. Matthew, as a boss clown desperately trying to keep things together as I, the more naïve disrupter, got bored, messed up scenes and generally played the fool. We leant into the smugness of the boss clown, the one who pretends they know what's going on but doesn't have a clue. We explored the attributes of the more naïve disrupter, the openness to the audience, the desire for disruption and improvisation. What do both clowns have in common? The love of the audience. This is what the clowns battle for, in their own different ways: for the attention, laughter and affection of the audience.

Because a clown show is nothing without an audience, we introduced them to the show early and included them in the process. Each Friday we opened the rehearsal room to anyone who wanted to see what we were up to, and this was where the clowns and the show really came alive. Because the clowns were genuinely competing for attention and support from a group of people the show became political in a new, original and extremely live way. Suddenly, the conflict between the clowns illuminated something of our own political turmoil that led to Trump and Brexit; the neoliberal versus the populist. We found something that felt very close to home, and that we felt ownership to explore. This was the moment we really discovered the form and content relationship. The smug hubris of the neoliberal silencing the protesting populist below him bites him badly when the populist wrestles control from him. The populist is driven by an insatiable appetite for attention and then power. Total power. This is the fertile ground for authoritarianism to emerge, as we explore in the second half of the show. Because we use clowning to get there it means that the audience are complicit in a unique and powerful way. The audience have been laughing, cheering, supporting, playing along this whole time until it's suddenly too late. We wanted a joyful complicity to turn into a stomach-turning realisation that what we've collectively created, what we've built into realisation, is a populist dictator.

Matthew Wells on the structure

Whilst making *Project Dictator* we were increasingly cognisant that although Britain under Johnson was showing worrying disregard for democratic values – and by extension artistic freedom – in comparison to those artists we talked to making work under autocratic and authoritarian regimes, we had the freedom to devise a show free from the threat of violence or persecution. It was therefore important that this reality be reflected within the structure of the piece.

This resulted in two central questions that guided our process: firstly, what kind of show would we make with absolute artistic freedom?

And secondly, what kind of theatre/art would an authoritarian regime sanction? The answers to these questions resulted in probably our most formally experimental show, with the show radically changing from the midpoint. This change is surprising and necessarily disorientating. In this way the structure of *Project Dictator* mirrors the sudden and confusing manner in which democracy can slide into autocracy.

Project Dictator was first performed at New Diorama Theatre, London on 29 March 2022. The cast and creative team were as follows:

Cast and Creatives

A Rhum + Clay production

Commissioned by New Diorama Theatre

By Hamish MacDougall, Julian Spooner and Matthew Wells
and devised by the company

Co-Directors and Performers: Julian Spooner and Matt Wells
Composer and Musician: Khaled Kurbeh
Co-Director: Hamish MacDougall
Set and Costume Designer: Blythe Brett
Lighting Designer: Simeon Miller
Associate Director: Mine Çerçi
Production Manager and Technical Stage Manager: Adam Jefferys
Sound Engineer: Ben Grant
Assistant Director: Sam Critchlow
Producer: Grace Dickson
Assistant Stage Manager: Moya Matthews
Assistant Designer: Dan Southwell
Assistant Producer: Rory Thomas-Howes
Lighting Programmer: Ben Garcia
Production Photography: Cesare De Giglio

Alterations and additions to the cast and creative team for the 2023 tour:

Musician: Sarah Spencer
Technical Stage Manager: Lauren Wedgeworth
Lighting Design Associate: Charly Dunford
Set and Costume Design Associate: Emily Nelson
Producer: Felicity Paterson

Blythe Brett – Set and Costume Designer

Blythe trained at the Royal Drawing School and Royal Welsh College of Music and Drama. She is a recipient of the Linbury Prize for Stage Design 2021 and Lord Williams Memorial Prize for Design 2020. Upcoming design credits include *This Much I Know* (Hampstead Theatre) and the Max Rayne Design Placement (National Theatre). Recent design credits include *Project Dictator* (New Diorama Theatre); *Who Killed My Father* (Tron Theatre); *Three Sisters* (LAMDA); *Get Happy* (Pleasance London); *Ariadne* and *Michelangelo Suite* (English Touring Opera). Associate design credits include *Vanya* (West End) and *KIN* (Gecko and National Theatre).

Mine Çerçi – Associate Director

After studying Theatre Studies at the Sorbonne and taking the two year acting course at École Jacques Lecoq, Mine joined Clout Theatre as a performer and a director. Two shows that she directed were nominated for Total Theatre Awards. Mine has translated the first ever Turkish edition of *Le Corps Poetique* by Jacques Lecoq. In Istanbul, she worked with private, state and municipal theatres as a freelance director. Since 2012 she has been running physical theatre workshops for professionals. She is currently teaching at the Identity School of Acting in London.

Sam Critchlow – Assistant Director

Sam is a theatre director and performer from the North West of England. Sam got their MA in Directing from Rose Bruford College Wigan in 2022 and is currently training at L'École Internationale de Théâtre Jacques Lecoq in France.

Grace Dickson – Producer (2022)

Grace Dickson is a Newcastle-born producer with a keen eye for powerful, socially relevant new writing. Grace works across the industry in roles including associate producer at Francesca Moody Productions (*An Oak Tree, Kathy and Stella Solve a Murder*, *Feeling Afraid as if Something Terrible is Going to Happen*); company producer for Lagahoo Productions and These Girls; accounts assistant/bookkeeper at Runaway Entertainment and co-founder of

HD General Management with Ameena Hamid. Her recent work is supported by the Stage One Bursary for New Producers. Credits include *Lady Dealer* (Roundabout, Edinburgh Fringe); *Glass Ceiling Beneath the Stars* (Pleasance, Edinburgh Fringe) with Bric à Brac Theatre; *SPLINTERED* (Soho Theatre); *Project Dictator* (New Diorama); *Move Fast and Break Things* (Summerhall, Edinburgh Fringe); *BOGEYMAN* (Pleasance Edinburgh Fringe); *Flushed* (Park Theatre) and *Belly Up* (Turbine Theatre).

Charly Dunford – Lighting Design Associate (2023)

Charly is a graduate from Liverpool Institute for Performing Arts and has recently won ALPD Michael Northern Award. Charly's credits include, as Lighting Designer: *Driftwood* (Pentabus), *Blood Harmony* (UK Tour), *this is not a crime – this is just a play* (Liverpool Everyman), *Vagina Cake* (Hope Mill Theatre), *Silla* (Leeds Opera Festival), *Little Red Robbin Hood* (Battersea Arts Centre), *Wild Swimming by Full Rogue* (Theatre on the Downs), *Séance* (The Station), *A Very Odd Birthday Party* (UK Tour), *Much Ado About Nothing* (Shakespeare North Playhouse). As Assistant Lighting Designer: *Cabaret* (Kit Kat Club at the Playhouse), *What's New Pussycat* (Birmingham Rep). As Relighter: *Vortex* (Russel Maliphant Dance Company), *How Not to Drown* (ThickSkin), *Shades of Blue* (Matsena Productions), *Good Grief* (Ugly Bucket). As Associate Lighting Designer: *Fleabag* (Sherman Theatre), *Curtain Up* (Theatr Clwyd), *Shades of Blue* (Matsena Productions UK Tour), *The Sorcerer's Apprentice* (Northern Stage), *STUFFED* (Ugly Bucket UK Tour).

Adam Jefferys – Production Manager and Technical Stage Manager (2022)

Adam is a lighting designer and production manager from Essex. He was previously the technical manager of the New Diorama Theatre. Recent production management credits include *Elephant* (Bush Theatre); *Pilot* (Summerhall); *Soon* (Summerhall); *Under the Kundè Tree* (Southwark Playhouse); *Philosophy of the World* (Cambridge Junction); *After The Act* (New Diorama) and *Everything Has Changed* (Pleasance). Recent lighting design credits include *It Is I*, *Seagull* (UK tour); *Please Love Me* (Pleasance); *Our Last First* – Offie Commendation (The Space); *Philosophy of the World* (Cambridge Junction); *Jekyll & Hyde* (Derby Theatre); *Everything Has Changed*

(Pleasance) and *Dorian* (Reading Rep). For Adam's portfolio: www.adamjefferys.com

Khaled Kurbeh – Composer and Musician

Khaled is a musician and composer living in Berlin. His projects span live performance and composition for theatre. He attended the Electroacoustic Composition classes of Prof. Kirsten Reese at UdK Berlin and graduated with an MA in Spatial Strategies from Kunsthochschule Berlin-Weißensee. His debut EP with oud player Raman Khalaf, 'Aphorisms', was released on Between Buttons label in 2017. His work has been performed at Münchner Kammerspiele, Munich, Synergy World Theater Festival, Novi Sad, Ableton Loop and XJAZZ Festival, Berlin, among others.

Hamish MacDougall – Co-writer and Co-director

Hamish is a theatre maker based in London. He works as a director, dramaturge and performer. For fifteen years Hamish has made award-winning work in the fields of theatre, comedy and performance art. His work has been presented at venues such as the Soho Theatre, New Diorama Theatre, the Southbank Centre, Battersea Arts Centre, Gaiety Theatre Dublin as well as touring to countries such as Germany, The Netherlands, Norway, Australia and USA. Recent work includes *The War of the Worlds* (Rhum and Clay/UK and international tour); *Buffy Revamped* (UK and international tour); *Project Alpine Tunnel (We Need to Talk About Fear and Death)* (CPT/Goldsmiths University); *The Narcissist* which Hamish co-wrote with Graham Dickson (BAC/Toomler Amsterdam/translated into Norwegian and performed at Sentralen Oslo); *Hammerhead* (Soho Theatre/Southbank Centre); *Soothing Sounds for Baby* (Soho Theatre). Hamish is also an associate of the Kandinsky Theatre Company and has co devised and performed in their shows *The Winston Machine*, *Dinomania*, *Still Ill*, *Dog Show* (New Diorama Theatre); and *Trap Street* (Schaubuhne Berlin and New Diorama). Awards include an Off West End Award for Best Ensemble and a Peter Brook Festival Award (both for *Dog Show*); Brighton Comedy Award and Pleasance Best Comedy Show (both for *Hammerhead*); Chortle Award for Innovation and a listing in the 2015 Guardian top ten shows across all art forms (both for *Soothing Sounds for Baby*). Hamish has also recently completed an MA in Art and Politics at Goldsmiths University.

Simeon Miller – Lighting Designer

Simeon has worked as a Lighting Designer since he graduated from Mountview Academy in 2010. He works across theatre, dance, musicals, 'gig theatre' and devised work. He enjoys contributing to new writing, especially socially and politically conscious work which amplifies oppressed and radical voices. Selected recent credits include *The Book of Will* (Queen's Theatre Hornchurch, Bolton Octagon and Shakespeare North Playhouse); *Ruckus* (Southwark Playhouse and Summerhall, Edinburgh); *Jekyll & Hyde* (Derby Theatre and Queen's Theatre Hornchurch); *Christmas in the Sunshine* (Unicorn Theatre); *Follow the Signs* (Soho Theatre); *The Poison Belt* (Jermyn Street Theatre); *Project Dictator* (New Diorama Theatre); *An Adventure* (Bolton Octagon); *Metamorphoses* (The Globe); *The Mob Reformers* (Lyric Hammersmith); *Subject Mater* (Edinburgh Fringe); *Black Holes* (international tour) and *High Rise eState of Mind* (UK tour). His full portfolio and credits can be found online at www.simeon.lighting

Felicity Paterson – Producer (2023)

Felicity Paterson is an independent theatre producer and senior producer for Rhum+ Clay. As producer, credits include *Everything Has Changed* (Rhum + Clay); *RICE!* (Omnibus Theatre and Wayang Kitchen); *Zeraffa Giraffa* (Omnibus Theatre and Little Angel Theatre); *MULE* (Omnibus Theatre, Gilded Balloon and UK tour); *The Little Prince* (Omnibus Theatre); *Hangmen Rehanged* (National Theatre Live, Kings College London and Omnibus Theatre); *SAD* (Omnibus Theatre); *Colour* (Omnibus Theatre and Lambeth Libraries); *Anonymous Anonymous* (Tressillian and The Space).

Sarah Spencer – Musician (2023)

Sarah is a composer and sound designer based in London and Berlin. She works across theatre, film, TV and installation. She has worked on a range of projects across film (*Tunnelen*, 2020), TV (*Sorgenfresser*, 2020), radio (*In His Kiss*, 2019) and sound installation (EMPRes Collective, 2021). As composer and lyricist, she worked on Smauel French published musical, *How to Save a Rock* (2020). She is resident composer for London-based theatre companies Freight Theatre and TheatreGoose, and co-director of cabaret collective Beware the Dogs.

Julian Spooner – Co-writer/Co-director and Performer

Julian is a multi-award winning actor, director, writer and co-artistic director of Rhum + Clay Theatre Company. He studied drama at the University of Bristol before training for two years at École Jacques Lecoq in Paris where he co-founded Rhum + Clay Theatre Company. Since 2010 he has acted as co-artistic director of the company and has co-created all their productions. Most notably he co-directed and performed in the critical smash hit *64 Squares*, directed the multi-award winning *TESTOSTERONE*, which has since toured across the world. In 2018, Julian made his solo performance debut in Dario Fo's *Mistero Buffo* in Edinburgh, where he won The Stage Award for acting excellence, and the show transferred to the main house at Arcola Theatre. In 2019 he co-created and co-directed *The War of the Worlds* which ran at the New Diorama for five sold out weeks and was a smash hit at the Fringe 2019. The production went on a mid-scale tour of the UK and the US in 2021. He co-created and directed the company's first work for young people *Everything Has Changed,* which transferred to the Southbank Centre. He has also toured the world playing the role of Ishmael in Plexus Polaire's acclaimed production of *Moby Dick.* He's a long-term collaborator with Shon Dale-Jones and Hoipolloi, having made *The Ladder* in 2019, they are developing a new work for screen. His comedy short film *Toby* was selected for film festivals across the globe, winning various awards. Next on the horizon, he will be co-director and performer in *GIANTS*, a co-production between Black Swan Theatre Company, National Theatre of Parramatta and Rhum + Clay.

His work has been performed in China, Taiwan, Kazakhstan, mainland Europe, Australia, Brazil, Venezuela, Canada and USA.

Website: www.julianspooner.co.uk

Lauren Wedgeworth – Technical Stage Manager (2023)

Lauren is a freelance stage manager and theatre maker. Stage management credits include *The Wetsuitman* (Foreign Affairs), *The Unicorn* (Arcola Theatre); *No Man's Island* (The Big House); *Under the Bridge*, a new solo show by Libby Liburd (developed as part of the Barbican Open Lab programme); *Everything Has Changed* (Rhum +

Clay) and *The Border Game* (Prime Cut Productions). Other credits include *The Wedding Speech* (Assistant Director); *Freshers* (Lighting and Set Designer); *Space Girls* (Writer and Director) and *Shakespeare in Lockdown: Lady Macbeth* (Director).

Matthew Wells – Co-writer/Co-director and Performer

Matt Wells is the co-artistic director of Rhum + Clay Theatre Company since 2011, as well as a freelance actor, director and educator. He graduated from École Jacques Lecoq in 2011, and holds a BA in Performances from the University of Western Sydney 2003. Recent credits include co-deviser, movement director and performer for *Everything Has Changed* (selected for the Southbank Centre 2023 Imagine Festival), co-deviser, movement director and performer in *The War of the Worlds* (included in 2019 British Council Showcase, with repeat UK and international tours); co-deviser and performer in *TESTOSTERONE* (British Council Showcase 2017, winner of best theatre show at Pleasance 2017, extensive UK and international tours); *64 Squares* (Underbelly Edinburgh sell-out show and UK national tour 2018). Upcoming credits include co-director and performer in *GIANTS*, a large-scale co-production between Western Australia state theatre company, Black Swan Theatre and the National Theatre of Parramatta.

Matt is also passionate about education and has extensive teaching credits, having most recently created and led workshops for the Old Vic, National Theatre, WAAPA and Sydney Festival, and University of Bournemouth amongst others. This work has taken him around the world after being invited to lead workshops in Australia, Germany, America, Kazakhstan, Canada, Brazil and Venezuela.

About Rhum + Clay

'A substantial body of work . . . super-smart' – Lyn Gardner, *The Guardian*

Rhum + Clay is led by artistic directors Julian Spooner and Matthew Wells, and was formed in 2010 at École Jacques Lecoq. Our work is created through a collaborative devised process, and always with a different creative ensemble. To date, the company has created ten new productions, all of which have been supported by Arts Council England. We have always been passionate about taking our work out to new audiences, as a result we have toured the UK and across the globe extensively.

Rhum + Clay's work stems from the belief that theatre is fundamentally an entertaining exercise in collective empathy, with theatre makers uniquely well-placed to generate a creative conversation with audiences about the world we live in and how we navigate it together.

Productions are collaboratively devised from a definitive departure point, whether an existing cultural artefact, such as a novel, photograph, story or an individual moment in our collective contemporary life, but always from something that feels enticing, urgent, and significant.

Rhum + Clay's most notable previous productions are the critical smash hit *The War of the Worlds*, which used Orson Welles' infamous 1938 radio broadcast to talk about fake news and disinformation. The ground-breaking *TESTOSTERONE* which explored masculinity through the eyes of a trans man in a men's changing room, solo-show *Mistero Buffo* which addressed the plight of the gig economy worker and won the prestigious Stage award for acting excellence, and *Everything Has Changed* commissioned in the height of COVID to respond to the challenges faced by young people, the show was critically acclaimed and later transferred to the Southbank Centre.

Rhum + Clay's next large-scale theatre production is *GIANTS*, a collaboration with Stephen Laughton and Kate Champion, and is a co-production with Australian partners Black Swan Theatre Company and National Theatre Parramatta. It is slated to open in 2025 and tour the UK and internationally in 2026/27.

Acknowledgements . . .

We'd like to acknowledge the wealth of stories and experience that we drew on to make this show, not only from our interviewees but from our collaborators. Instrumental in this was Khaled Kurbeh, who created the show alongside us and provided a wonderful original score. Also, Mine Çerçi with her fabulous associate direction and insight into the subject matter (and for laughing at us being stupid).

A devised production stands on the shoulders of those in the room who make it. We'd like to acknowledge the contributions of designer Blythe Brett, assistant director Sam Critchlow, lighting designer Simeon Miller, producer Grace Dickson and production manager Adam Jefferys.

Also, theatre cannot exist without an empty space for it to occupy. We are indebted to New Diorama Theatre in London for a decade of unwavering support of Rhum + Clay, and for commissioning a bonkers clown show about authoritarianism.

Thank you to David Byrne and Sophie Wallis for believing in us from the very beginning. Also, Will Young, Reece Mcmahon and Jo Langdon for their support on *Project Dictator*.

Our thanks go to our unbelievably supportive board of trustees: Anthony Alderson, Nadia Newstead, Sophie Wallis and Sarah Wilson-White. You've got our backs like no others.

We'd also like to thank Guy J Sanders for his incredible design on both the poster and our logo, as well as Cesare De Giglio for his photography.

On a personal note, Julian would like to thank Laura Carniel Benin, Sophie Cullen, Cassidy Cullen-Spooner, Brenda Hamlet and Paul Spooner.

Matthew would like to thank Ella Cox and Hazel Lucy Hirons.

Hamish would like to thank Bernadette Buckley, David Labi, Susan MacDougall and Roxanne Peak Payne.

Dedicated to all the international artists who we spoke to in the making of this work. The sharing of their experience of living and working under authoritarianism had a profound impact. For their safety they remain anonymous.

Project Dictator

(or 'Why Democracy is Overrated and I Don't Miss It At All')

'I am condemned to resist.'

An anonymous artist living under censorship

Cast of Characters (in order of appearance)

Kevin Kevinson, *musician*
Martin Wallace / Performer A
Jeremy Smithson / Performer B

*NB: in the restaging of this play the names of these characters should
be assigned to the performers who play them. Take the first letter of
the actual performer's name and create a character name from it,
e.g. if your performer is called Chris Hawkins their character could
be called Colin Haverton. The performers playing these roles can be
any gender, race or age.*

*For this edition we will reference the original character names of
Kevin, Martin and Jeremy.*

Director's Note on Act One

The inspiration behind this half was to create the freest, maddest, most bonkers political clown satire that we could. Having spoken to artists all over the world who weren't afforded the freedom that we often take for granted in the UK, we decided to embrace that freedom; to create something that is formally, thematically and performatively free in every way.

In terms of narrative chronology, Act One is set in the 'now' and should always be performed as so. The show was created in 2022 in Britain and so the aesthetics, props and characterisation draw on a political landscape in the long shadow of Brexit and the cost of living crisis. When restaging the play, it's important that Act One reflects whatever time it is performed in. Fortunately (for the script/unfortunately for the world), we imagine most of it will be timeless; an endless struggle between populist and status quo/neoliberal.

This first half should function as a piece of clown theatre, by which we mean a piece of theatre *made* by clowns rather than just clowning within a piece of theatre. It's a subtle difference but an essential one. It means we made the first half from the perspective of a clown, certain artistic choices that we wouldn't make as theatre makers, we have made from the state of mind of both Martin and Jeremy. It also allowed us to make a satire from clown play without being heavy handed, with the status quo/neo-liberal smarminess of Martin wrestling and shouting with the brash, bold and 'fun' populism of Jeremy. A recipe that often ends in despair and disaster, laying the groundwork for Act Two.

Because Act One is a piece of clown theatre you should see the clown's fingerprints on every aspect of the design and costume; from the cardboard props made in haste at home, to the gaffer tape moustache that Jeremy dons as the leader, to the botched lighting states, to Martin's faux intellectual glasses, it should all feel and look DIY and be dripping with comedic potential. It's not that they're trying to make it look bad, it's just that they can't do any better. Martin thinks he's written a Tom Stoppard, but he's misinterpreted the quantity over quality rule, and Jeremy just wants a better deal for himself and ultimately to become the centre of attention. For him, like many political leaders, it's really all about *him*.

Act One Reader

Because much of the first act is made from competing perspectives, we decided to put footnotes from different perspectives. Hopefully this makes the play more fun to read, easier to stage, and gives a sense of what might be behind certain moments.

Here are the different keys for the footnotes:

Rhum + Clay (R+C): from the makers of *Project Dictator* on our intentions, different ways to play certain moments, and how to stage the play *Project Dictator*.

Martin Wallace (MW): on how to stage his play *How to Solve the Problem . . . (s)*.

Jeremy Smithson (JS): on how to stage his fun version and how to get the better of Martin.

Martin (left) and Jeremy (right) on the campaign trail. Note the hastily made cardboard door prop. Photography: Cesare De Giglio.

Jeremy protests with his homemade megaphone helmet. Photography: Cesare De Giglio.

Jeremy as the new leader. Photography: Cesare De Giglio.

Bang. Photography: Cesare De Giglio.

Act One

Show Voice   Welcome to the show. Please remember to turn off your mobile phones. This show will last four hours and thirty seven minutes with no interval. Enjoy.[1]

Kevin *plays a fast classical intro.* **Martin** *enters centre stage. Thumbs up to* **Kevin**. **Kevin** *stops the music to hear what* **Martin** *is saying.* **Martin** *looks around agitated that the music has stopped.*

Martin   No, no, no, no . . .

Kevin *starts again.* **Martin** *arrives at the downstage centre and gestures to stop* **Kevin**, *who stops playing.*

Martin   Welcome everybody to what I hope will be a momentous night[2] at the theatre.

Martin *gestures with hands expansively;* **Kevin** *misunderstands this as a cue to start playing again.* **Martin** *gestures for him to stop.*

Martin (*stage whisper*)   Kevin, when I do this (*he gestures*) it means stop. When I do this (*he does another gesture*) it means start.

Kevin *starts playing music.* **Martin** *stops him.* **Jeremy** *pokes his head from behind the curtain stage left.*

Jeremy   Is everything okay?

Martin   Yes, it's fine.

Jeremy   Good luck.

Jeremy *thumbs up to* **Kevin** *who misunderstands this as a gesture to start playing,* **Martin** *gestures for him to stop.* **Jeremy** *retreats back behind the curtain.*

Martin   Kevin! Just take your hands away.

---

[1] The voice for the Show Voice should sound like a venue announcement. It is then repurposed for the second half but should sound the same
[2] MW: If it is a matinee or for some godforsaken reason you're being forced to perform in the daytime please feel free to change evening to an appropriate time. This is the only improvisation allowed in my script.

Kevin *sheepishly removes his hands from the keyboard.* **Martin** *moves towards the audience.*

Martin   Right, where were we? As you're all probably aware, my name is Martin Wallace, and I am a polymath of the theatre. Some of you have probably seen some of my work before. Some of you maybe haven't. Welcome if so. Anyway, I won't mess around, and I'll cut to the chase. This time I thought it was right to tackle the big one. Yes, that's right this is my state of the nation play. It is entitled *How to Solve the Problem . . .(s).*[3] Okay that's enough of that. Now a few trigger warnings. This is an incredibly complex piece of work; it will be dense and difficult to follow. But as we know, theatre isn't always meant to be enjoyable. The hero of the play, Tobias Wilson Jones. He's a young, charismatic, political renegade. Think Emmanuel Macron meets . . . Jesus Christ. Kevin will be on the keys here. (**Kevin** *begins to play and* **Martin** *stops him.*) And my supporting actor, Jeremy Smithson, will be playing everything else.

Jeremy *emerges from behind the curtain and amiably approaches the audience.*

Jeremy   Hello, every –

Martin   Don't speak. Just get into position.

Martin *spins* **Jeremy** *around to face the curtain. On the back of his boiler suit are stitched the words 'Everything Else'.*

Martin   Okay right. Finally, we are ready to start our play. I hope you enjoy, *How to Solve the Problem . . . (s)*

Martin *goes behind the closed curtain.* **Kevin** *begins playing music.* **Jeremy** *spins around to face the audience. He is holding a cardboard replica of the United Kingdom.*[4] *He pulls it apart revealing a map in two parts. He hasn't anticipated the length of the voiceover and fills his stage time by moving the map in a dramatic fashion.*

---

[3] R+C: The electronic title screen at the top of the stage should indicate the title of Martin's play. It should scroll either comedically too fast or too slowly.
[4] R+C: If you're staging this play in another country, do feel free to make a cardboard cut out of said place. It's important that the show feels relevant to the time and place.

Voiceover   The nation is divided. Broken supply chains. Empty supermarket shelves. Endless queues of people. The energy crisis. Violence. Chaos. The nation has lost its voice.[5] Who can put this country back together? The nation is in desperate need of leadership. Enter our hero, Tobias. Walking down a rainy street. Like many of the population, completely lost and without a clue.[6]

Martin *enters as Tobias Wilson Jones, he is walking down a street reacting to mimed rain and wind.* **Kevin** *cues the sound of thunder and rain.*

Martin   I'm completely lost and I don't have a clue. I know I was born to do something special but what is it? If only someone could tell me the way.

Jeremy *bumps into* **Martin** *with so much gusto it nearly knocks them both to the floor.*

Martin   Excuse me, sir. Where are you going?

Jeremy   Sorry, I'm late for work.

Martin   Where do you work?

Jeremy   At the Amazon warehouse.[7] If I'm late they'll kill me.

Martin   Hang on, wait!

They both turn into a new space; the Amazon warehouse. **Jeremy** *is running all over the stage scanning his box. He's desperately trying to recreate the atmosphere of a busy warehouse.* **Martin** *remains centre stage taking in the space.*

Martin   Wow, look at this place. Look at all these thousands of workers. Beavering away. You sir, can I speak to you?

---

[5] MW: At this point I made sure Jeremy does an exaggerated silent scream. Literal visual metaphors are your strongest ally in this piece of political drama.
[6] R+C: The tone of this voiceover is best being bombastic and just on the line of being completely ridiculous.
[7] R+C : The electronic sign should leave a comically long pause before revealing the word AMAZON.

Jeremy   No, I'm incredibly busy, sorry.[8]

Martin   What about you, madam?

Jeremy   I'm sorry, I'm very busy. I can't.

Martin   What about you, sir?

Jeremy   Sorry, I only get one break and I really need the toilet.

Martin   You only have one break? How long is your shift?

Jeremy   Fifteen hours.

Martin   What, you work fifteen hours, and you only get one toilet break?

Jeremy   Yep, that's right. I need the toilet.

Martin   But what's on your mind?

Jeremy   The toilet.

Martin   But what do you want out of life?

Jeremy   I need the toilet.

Martin   But what else?

Jeremy   Toilet.[9]

Martin   Wait. I can see something.[10] A future.[11] A better future. Imagine the future where you can get as many toilet breaks as you want.

Jeremy   What?

---

[8] JS: You're gonna have to do a lot of multi rolling in this piece if you're doing this part. Try and switch between different people using the bent back/straight back technique. Going from high voice to low voice is also a good one. There's no such thing as a small role, only small actors.

[9] MW: Jeremy can get fixated on a line sometimes. If he gets caught in a loop I often just skip over to the next bit.

[10] MW: Here you're not actually seeing something, it's a vision. Try and imagine the best thing you've never seen, and place it beyond the fourth wall . . . we'll come back to that later

[11] R+C: Here the electronic sign can say THE FUTURE. Accompany it with some digital future sounds, like PC music.

Martin   A world where this technology works for you.

Jeremy   Really?

Martin   They can do better things. Robots should be doing their jobs.

Martin *tries to take* **Jeremy**'s *box, but* **Jeremy** *grips onto it.*

Jeremy   No. No. Don't. Don't take my job.[12]

Martin (*stage whisper*)   That's not the line, Jeremy.

Jeremy   Don't take my job! I've got a wife and three children.

They wrestle over the box, **Martin** *is becoming increasingly frustrated.*

Martin   Jeremy . . . I'm emancipating you. You're supposed to agree with me.

Jeremy (*aside*)   I'm trying to make it more truthful.

Martin   Fine, you can retrain and do something else.

Jeremy   What?

Martin   I don't know, Jeremy. Something else. Google it.

Jeremy   That's not very specific!

Martin *stamps on* **Jeremy**'s *foot and manages to get the box off him.*

Jeremy   OW!

Pause.

Martin   Wow, I feel like I really connected with that person.

Jeremy *doesn't say the following line so* **Martin** *hits* **Jeremy** *with the box*

---

[12] R+C: The idea here is that Jeremy has gotten carried away with his character and forgotten the blocking of the scene
JS: I just think about Ken Loach when I'm doing this bit. Really get into the social realism of it.

Jeremy   Why don't you tell me more about this vision for the future?

Martin   Yes. Yes. Yes. Yes[13] . . . Imagine a future where everyone has the job they want.

Jeremy   Really?

Martin   Everyone can buy the house of their dreams.

Jeremy   Amazing!

Martin   Better education. Better healthcare. A better future.

Jeremy   How do we get there?

Martin   I don't know yet.[14]

Jeremy   You've got to go and tell people this.

Martin   Me?

Jeremy   You've solved my problem, now you should go out and solve more . . . problems.

A spotlight highlights **Martin** *in a heroic pose. He pushes* **Jeremy** *backwards out of the light.* **Jeremy** *goes and gets the props ready for the campaign trail. During the voiceover* **Jeremy** *is clanking around trying to prep for the next scene.* **Martin** *is growing increasingly frustrated at the distraction.*

Voiceover   Tobias on that day realised his fate. He realised that he needed to help people. And the only way he could do that was by becoming a politician. Through his sheer intelligence he shot up the ranks of a major political party. But he couldn't solve the problems yet because first he needed to become the leader. And to do that he had to convince the people on the campaign trail.

---

[13] R+C: Martin is waiting for the lighting technician to cue to the next lighting state and so is repeating the cue line 'yes'.

[14] MW: Don't worry you will find out how, I just want to pepper the insights through the show to keep the audience engaged

Jeremy *appears with a tiny door,* **Martin** *knocks on various doors in different positions with different people behind them. Behind the third one* **Martin** *poses for a photo with* **Jeremy**.

Jeremy *runs on stage with a football.*

Martin   Footy! On the head.[15]

Jeremy *throws a football for* **Martin** *to head it back. They take another photo.*

Jeremy *gets a ribbon and holds it in different places for* **Martin** *to cut with giant scissors.*

Martin   I now open this hospital! (*SFX applause.*) This school! (*Applause.*) This motorway! (*Applause.*) This children's hospital!

Jeremy *passes* **Martin** *a baby.* **Martin** *sees the baby and kisses it.* **Jeremy** *throws another baby to* **Martin**. **Martin** *is confused and takes the baby. This is repeated with more babies.* **Martin** *ends up holding six babies and tries to kiss them all on the head.* **Jeremy** *throws a ball by accident and it hits* **Martin** *in the face. The babies cascade to the ground. A photo is taken at that exact moment.*

Jeremy *runs to get tree branches.* **Martin** *gets the helmet and trowel.*

Martin   With this soil I plant this commemorative tree –

Jeremy *enthusiastically opens out to a large tree and whacks* **Martin** *in the face with the branches.*

Martin *grabs the branch off* **Jeremy**. *He hits* **Jeremy** *with the branch and there is a flash. Another photo is taken. He is frantically whipping* **Jeremy** *with a branch, chastising him for his mistakes. Over the beating the following voiceover plays.*

Voiceover   Tobias had charmed the people with his grace, his empathy, and his natural charisma. Finally, the country had a politician who was willing to listen. And in his keynote speech he would begin to tell the country how to solve the problems!

---

[15] R+C: For a reference point for a performance style look to Rishi Sunak pretending to be a normal person out and about.

Jeremy *has disappeared backstage,* **Martin** *realises it is his cue to come back on stage for his victory speech. He throws the helmet on the ground and picks up a microphone.*

Martin   Citizens of the nation, good evening. It is an absolute honour and a privilege to stand here tonight as your newly elected leader.

Kevin *misses his cue to trigger applause.* **Martin** *cues* **Kevin** *for the SFX of audience applause. He then cues him to stop it.*

Martin   More than this I am frankly relieved that I, Tobias Wilson Jones, can finally get down to the hard work of solving the problem . . .s. (*SFX audience applause.*) Ever since one fateful night ten years ago when I visited an Amazon warehouse, I realised that my calling in life was not about helping myself but helping others. That's who I'm in it for, you, the people of this country. The people that I love. And I love this country. A country of spirit. Hope. Intelligence. Compassion. Togetherness. Innovation. Determination. Education. But I know what you are all thinking. How am I going to solve the problems? Well, let me tell you now –

During this last line **Jeremy** *has entered wearing a helmet with a megaphone attached to it. He speaks through the amplified megaphone.*[16]

Jeremy   Absolute bullshit!

Martin   Jeremy?! Is that you? What are you doing? What is that on your head?

Jeremy   I'm not Jeremy, mate. I'm just a member of the public listening to your speech. Why don't you carry on?

Martin   This is completely unprofessional.

---

[16] R+C: It's important that Jeremy appears from a different place than from where he exited, and most importantly all of this initial dialogue must take place with Jeremy in the stalls with the audience. He has become the voice of the people.

Jeremy   Jesus Christ, this is pretty boring, isn't it? Does anyone you know what he's banging on about? I haven't got a clue.

Martin   Okay, okay. SHOW STOP!

Jeremy   YOU CAN'T SHOW STOP THIS, MATE. THIS SHOW IS NOT STOPPING.

Jeremy *jumps onto the stage next to* **Martin** *and talks directly to the audience.*

Jeremy   This guy is ridiculous, he's not even a real person!

Martin   Of course I'm a real person, Jeremy.

Jeremy   He's not a real politician. He's just put a suit and tie on and he's pretending to speak to you, the people.

Martin   Yes, Jeremy that's because I'm an actor *playing* a politician –

Jeremy   He admits it!

Martin   Just ignore him.

Jeremy   Oh, just ignore me. Classic. It's what he's been doing for years! He makes promises and he breaks them. He's betrayed me. The people. He's a liar and he's a traitor. He's a liar and a traitor!

Martin   To the dressing room. Now! Kevin, play something!

Kevin *starts to play and is stopped by* **Jeremy**.

Jeremy   Don't listen to him, Kevin. I'm staying right here.

Jeremy *lies down on the stage and goes limp.*

You are going to have to remove me by force in front of all these people.

Martin *looks around despairingly, he then grabs* **Jeremy**'s *foot and begins to drag him up stage towards the curtain.*

Jeremy   Look at this! This is what he's like. Are you seeing this? Can someone film this?! Film it!

Martin   Stop talking to them!

Martin *is frantically gesturing to the audience.*

Jeremy   Why?

Martin   When you're acting you pretend that they're not there.

Jeremy   But they are there!

Martin   There's a fourth wall, Jeremy! A fourth wall!

Jeremy   A four what?

Martin   This, look.

Martin *goes towards the audience and gestures at the space between stage and audience.*

It's a wall that you can't go through.

Jeremy   Oh, is there? Is there really?

Jeremy *goes up to the space that* **Martin** *has mimed and touches it whilst making a knocking noise through the megaphone.*

Jeremy   Oh, there is you know, he's right! I wonder if there's a door . . .

Jeremy *makes knocking noises along the length of the stage until he finds a mime door and 'creaks' it open. He parades in front of the audience in their space.*

Jeremy   There it is, found it! I've done it, I'm on the other side of the fourth wall! Woohoo!

Martin   Let me give you an acting lesson. You're such an amateur! A professional doesn't talk to the audience. You talk *at* them . . . and slightly above their heads.

Jeremy   This is what we're sick of, isn't it?! We are sick of being talked down to, undermined, condescended to, aren't we?[17] We are sick of playing ninety-nine per cent of all the characters in this script, aren't we?

Jeremy *is whipping up the crowd.*

And we're sick of him (*points at* **Martin**), aren't we?

Jeremy *joins the audience in the stalls again.*

Jeremy (*starting a chant*)   No more play! No more play!

Martin *is panicked and tries to shout over the crowd.*[18]

Martin   Okay. Okay. Okay! Jeremy –

Jeremy *is breathing heavily through his megaphone.*

Martin   Jeremy, can you stop doing that –

Jeremy   I'm breathing, Martin, I have to.

Martin   Look, I'm sorry . . . Okay?

Jeremy   That's a start.

Martin   I do . . . overwork you.

Jeremy   Yes.

Martin   I do under-appreciate you.

Jeremy   Correct.

Martin   I have underpaid you.

Jeremy   He has *never* paid me!

Martin   Look, that isn't the point, what I really should be doing is . . . admiring your amazing prop-making skills.

Jeremy *is taken aback by this unexpected praise.*

Jeremy   Oh . . . Thanks. Do you like it?

---

[17] R+C: The success of this scene depends on Jeremy winning the audience over to his side. At this moment do leave space for them to make affirmative noises. This needs to build to them chanting 'no more show'.

[18] R+C: Both performers need to allow the chanting to build to a cacophony until Martin manages to cut through.

Martin   It's phenomenal. Maybe we could use it in the show?

Jeremy   What? Really?

Jeremy *is slowly walking onto the stage to join* **Martin**.

Jeremy   Thanks . . . It's a bike helmet . . . With a megaphone attached to it.

Martin   Really? And you made it?

Jeremy   Yes, look. Just put cable ties on the back there.

Martin   That's so clever.

Jeremy   Thanks, I didn't think you'd like it.

Martin   Can I try it?

Slight pause as **Jeremy** *is wondering whether to trust* **Martin**. *He then quickly decides to give him a go and starts to take the megaphone helmet off his head.*

Jeremy   Sure. It's adjustable as well.

Martin   So you just put it on your head?

Jeremy   Yep. Just pop it on here, adjust it for your larger head.

Martin   And you do the clips like this?

Jeremy   That's it.

Martin   And you just adjust it here? And you speak in here?[19]

Jeremy   You got it.

Martin (*in megaphone and suddenly changing from calm to furious*)   THIS. IS. MY. SHOW! DO YOU UNDERSTAND? MINE! NOT YOURS! MINE! MY STAGE, MY LIGHTS, MY AUDIENCE . . . AND MY FUCKING KEVIN! NOW PISS OFF AND WAIT FOR YOUR NEXT SCENE.

---

[19] MW: Jeremy is such an idiot.

Jeremy *storms off behind the curtain and exits to the dressing room.*

Martin (*calming down and to the audience*)   Apologies, everyone. Clearly Jeremy is a little bit delusional. He's not doing very well and last night I found him crying. But that's private. So, let's keep that between me and you. You've all paid good money so the show must go on –

Jeremy *re-enters with another identical megaphone helmet.*

Jeremy   The revolution lives on! We cannot be stopped.[20]

Martin   Oh my god, he's got another one.

Jeremy   That's right!

Martin   How many more have you got back there?

Jeremy   Oh, wouldn't you like to know.

Martin   You've lost the plot.

Jeremy   At least you're listening to me now.

Martin   At least you're listening to *me*!

They begin to argue with each other whilst shouting through the megaphones,[21] *finally* **Martin** *interrupts . . .*

Martin   Okay, fine! Wait here.

Martin *exits through the curtains to the dressing room area.*

Jeremy   Did you see that? He just completely lost it.

Martin *re-enters in a rage with a huge script in a binder.*

Martin   Have you even *read* this?

Jeremy   What is it?

Martin   IT'S THE SCRIPT.

Jeremy   Is it?

---

[20] JS: Of course I made extras. How many? You'll never know.
[21] R+C: When staging this make sure both actors are saying actual things but just speaking over each other. If you get both megaphones screaming into each other it's a lovely image.

Martin   Come and look at this.

They both go to look at the script at the same time and bash megaphones. They try again with the same result.

Oh for god's sake. You go in first and read it. What does that say?

Jeremy *struggles with his megaphone helmet, just about jostling it in a position in which he can read the page.*

Jeremy   'How to Solve the Problems' by Martin Wallace.

Martin   And . . .?

Jeremy   Draft 42.

Martin   Exactly! I have given my life to this. I've spent a decade making what I consider to be a perfect, relevant drama. I wrote it and I know what I am doing.

Jeremy   I just think it's a bit boring.[22] (*A beat.* **Martin** *stares at* **Jeremy**, *aghast.*) I just think it could be a bit more fun. Martin? Martin? Martin?

Martin   Fun?

Jeremy   Yes, fun. You know like . . . Whey! We're having a fun night.

Martin   Fun?

Jeremy   Yeah, because to be honest, Martin. I think they're here to have fun. (**Jeremy** *is gesturing towards the audience.*)

Martin   No they're not.

Jeremy   Um. I think they are. (*Looks towards the audience.*) Can I get some lights on them? Hey, what's your name?

The selected audience member number 1 gives their name.

---

[22] R+C: This is a huge insult for Martin. The actor should freeze when he hears the word 'boring'. It's incomprehensible that his script is 'boring'.

Jeremy   Nice to meet you. (*Name of audience member.*) I'm Jeremy, that's Martin. Do you like fun things?

Audience Member 1 response.

Jeremy   What kind of fun things do you like?

Audience Member 1 response.

Jeremy   Would you prefer to be doing (*Insert audience response.*) than watching Martin's play?[23] Great! You see, Martin? People want fun.

Martin   Fine, fine. Okay, okay. I get it! I get it! The public and Jeremy have spoken! Everyone's a critic. All those sleepless nights where I stayed up agonising over how to structure a relevant political drama? I shouldn't have had to worry when I could have just added. (*Insert audience suggestion.*) Let's flush it down the toilet and have some fun, shall we?

Martin *takes the script and shows it to* **Jeremy** *for him to read.*

Martin   You see this bit, what does it say?

Jeremy   The press conference.

Martin   And what happens in the press conference?

Jeremy (*reading*)   The leader answers difficult and complicated questions from the press.

Martin   Difficult and complicated questions . . . Do you think you can make that fun?

Jeremy   Yes. We can try. Can't we! (*Implores the audience to cheer and support.*)

Martin   Oh you do, do you? Great, brilliant. Can't get any worse, can it? I give up. I've been publicly humiliated, my work is apparently worthless, what's the point? This is your show now, Jeremy, you do it.

---

[23] R+C: It's important Jeremy gets people on side in this bit. Don't be afraid to really nudge them over to support Jeremy in any way possible.

Martin *thrusts the huge script into* **Jeremy**'s *hands.*

Jeremy   What. Really? Now?

Martin   Yes. Now.

Jeremy   So, does that mean that I'm the leader?

Martin   Yep.

Jeremy   And so that means that you're playing *everything else*?

Martin   Sure.[24]

Jeremy   Wow. Wow, all right. Wow. Okay, let's do it. Thanks, Martin! The press conference. Oh, wow I've got so many ideas! Wait here!

Jeremy *sprints through the curtain off stage leaving* **Martin** *and the audience alone.*

Martin (*speaking to the audience member number 1*)   Just to let you know, whatever happens from here, it's on you.

Jeremy *comes bursting through the curtain back onto the stage with a huge bin on wheels with 'Jeremy's ideas' written on it.*[25]

Jeremy   Woohoo. Okay! So many ideas. So where do we start . . . Okay, okay, so I'm playing the leader now, right?

Martin *nods,* **Jeremy** *pops on some glasses on his face. They're broken aviators.*

Jeremy   That's a start. And you're playing?

Martin   Everything else.

Jeremy   So, that means you're playing the press, are you? Oh cool. Stick these on. (**Jeremy** *passes* **Martin** *some joke shop glasses with accompanying moustache.*) Right, Kevin . . . new show, new energy . . . I've got you a hat! (**Jeremy** *hands*

---

[24] MW: If I seem manically positive after having my dreams shattered, it's only because I'm so convinced Jeremy is going to fuck this up royally.

[25] JS: I added a huge amount of 'flair' onto the ideas box such as tassels.

Kevin *a jester's hat.*)[26] Oh, I've got a box for the press box, come stand on this, Martin! (**Jeremy** *gets a box out that says 'Press'*) Now I need a microphone. (*Picks up a microphone.*) So this is . . . Oh wow, is that my voice? Amazing. Let's have a look at the press conference lighting. (*Lights for* **Martin***'s press conference come on.*) Yeah, that's pretty boring . . . (*To the audience.*) Shall we have some more colour? Yeah! Let's get some colour up in this joint! That's better, ooh can you make them move?[27] Woohoo yeah, here we go! Ohh Kevin, what music did we have for the press conference? (**Kevin** *plays the serious theme.*) No, no, stop, stop. Stop that. Tell you what, go onto my Spotify playlist. It's called 'Jeremy's Fun House: Fun Timez'. 'Times' with a z at the end. Okay, great! Oh, what about the sign? (*The sign says Press Conference.*) Can we make that more fun? (*Sign becomes fun but disjointed.*) Yes, look at that! Press Conferenc . . . e!

Martin   *This* is boring, Jeremy.

Jeremy   Umm excuse me, Martin but this is part of the handover, can you let me do my job? Actually, Martin you also need a mic. (*Gets one and hands it to him.*) Can you speak into it?

Martin   Hello, I'm the press.

Jeremy   Kevin, can we do something fun with the voice?[28] Again, Martin.

Martin (*voice high pitched*)   Hello, I'm the . . . Oh for god's sake.

Jeremy   That's amazing! Okay, stop the lights, stop everything. I need to get ready.

Jeremy *runs backstage to put on his costume.*

---

[26] JS: If you know Kevin, you'd know how hilarious he looks in this hat.
[27] R+C: If you've got moving lights at your disposal, make them move around like the 20th Century Fox opening titles, if not make the lights do something a bit jazzy and cheesy.
[28] R+C: This is an audio effect on the mic to make the speaker's voice sound cartoonishly high pitched.

(*On mic.*) Okay, here we go. Okay, Martin, are you ready?

Martin (*not on mic*)   Yes.

Jeremy   Kevin, are you ready? (*Silence.*) I'll take that as a yes. Audience, are you ready? (*Response.*) Hit it!

Bonnie Tyler's 'I Need A Hero' blasts through the speakers, **Jeremy** *emerges from behind the curtains dressed as The Leader[29] with a hand-held smoke machine and loving the applause. He runs into the audience and begins high fiving them, he then slides across the stage on the ideas bin.* **Jeremy** *starts a chant with the audience.*

When I say Press, you say Conference! Press! (*Audience: Conference.*) Press! (*Audience: Conference.*)

Jeremy *cuts the music just as Bonnie Tyler belts out 'I need a Hero!'*

Welcome to the press conference! Question one . . .

Martin   How are you going to put –

Jeremy   Hold on, hold on. Kevin, could we have a drum roll before each question? Question one. (*Low energy drum roll.*) Yeah Kevin, could we have it with a bit more oomph behind it. You know, more energy. (*Higher energy drum roll.*) Whey okay! Question one.

Martin   How are you going to put downward pressure on inflation?

Jeremy (*pause as he genuinely tries to decipher the question*) I don't have a fucking clue what that means, next question!

Martin   What are you going to do about the current energy crisis?

Jeremy   Well . . . I'll tell ya how I'm gonna solve that one, by getting some goddamn energy in this room, am I right?! Kevin, track 3!

---

[29] JS: I was very much inspired by a cross between Freddie Mercury, Dr Stangelove and Mussolini (with sequins). Use gaffer tape for moustache.

Kevin *cues a disco track,* **Jeremy** *starts throwing balloons into the audience then begins to teach the audience the 'funky chicken'.*

Jeremy (*to the audience*)   Everybody, move your left elbow up and down, now your right elbow up and down, now both elbows up and down, it's the funky chicken! The funky chicken! We're all doing the funky chicken! The funky chick –

Martin *leaves his position and gets* **Kevin** *to cut the music dead.*

Jeremy   Martin, what the hell?!

Martin   The point of this scene is that you, *The Leader*, has to *answer* the questions.

Jeremy   Which I am doing!

Martin   Do you even understand the questions?

Jeremy   Uh . . . yes.[30] Hey, you know what. I don't like this press. (*Turns to the audience.*) They are so negative aren't they . . . There's all this positive energy over here (*Motioning to the audience.*) and all this negative energy over here. (*His hand settles on* **Martin**'s *face, before turning his attention on him.*) How about trying to be a little bit more positive?[31]

Martin   That's not how this works.

Jeremy   So negative! Why don't you just lighten up?

Martin   It's a serious scene!

Jeremy   It doesn't have to be, Martin! Come on, let's try again. (**Jeremy** *pushes* **Martin** *back onto the press box.*) Ask me a positive question.

Martin   There aren't any in the script.

---

[30] MW: Jeremy definitely doesn't understand any of these questions.

[31] R+C: It's good to see this as a turning point for Jeremy's character. As a populist he doesn't like 'difficult' and 'negative' attitudes towards him. We should start to see a little bit of the populist bully begin to appear in some of Jeremy's tone and physicality, needs to start small to have somewhere to go. For some inspiration look at how Trump compères his press conferences: https://www.youtube.com/watch?v=jtl5XK7QP38

Jeremy   Make one up then!

Martin   I certainly don't make things up.

Jeremy   Last chance, going . . . going . . . gone! You're fired. Let's get someone else. (**Jeremy** *snatches the microphone from* **Martin** *and takes a notepad out of his ideas box.*) Could we get some lights up on this audience?

Jeremy *approaches an audience member.*

Jeremy   Excuse me, what's your name?

Audience Member 2 response.

Jeremy   Do you have any experience in the press at all?

Audience Member 2 response.[32]

Jeremy   Perfect! (**Jeremy** *hands the audience member the notepad and microphone.*) Read this for me when I point at you . . . Okey! Next question from the press . . .

Kevin *does a drum roll and* **Jeremy** *points at the audience member.*

Audience Member (*reading from the notepad*)   The show is a lot better now that you're the leader, can it stay like this? Also, I really love your costume.

Jeremy   Well! I don't even need to answer those questions! I think that's pretty self explanatory, am I right?! Let's have a big round of applause for the press!

Jeremy *takes the notepad and microphone back and gives them to* **Martin**.

Jeremy   Okay, Martin? Positive questions now, yeah?

Martin   Yeah . . . positive.

Jeremy   You've learned from that, yeah?

---

[32] R+C: If the audience member says yes to this question then Jeremy needs to move onto someone else with a sense of, 'Sorry, you're over qualified'. Once Jeremy finds someone that says they have no experience in the press he can use them for his pre-written questions.

Martin   Yep, got it.

Jeremy   Okay! Next question from the press!

Kevin *does a drum roll and cymbal crash.* **Jeremy** *is waiting in earnest as* **Martin** *silently reads the question on the notepad.* **Martin** *then scrunches the questions and throws them at* **Jeremy**.

Martin (*into the mic*)   What are you going to do about climate change?

Jeremy   Great question.

Jeremy *is staring intently at* **Martin**, *he then turns towards* **Kevin**.

Jeremy   Kevin, play something serious on the keys for me . . .

Kevin *begins to play a melancholic refrain on the piano.* **Jeremy** *begins to feign fear and horror, gasping and groping at his face.*

Jeremy   Climate change! (*Gasps.*) So much change! In the climate. What are we going to do?! AH! I've got it.

Jeremy *feigns a lightbulb moment, clears his throat and brings the microphone to produce many fart noises into the microphone.*[33]

Martin   Jeremy, Jeremy. Jeremy, stop it. This is horrible.

Jeremy's *fart noises build in intensity and he chases* **Martin** *off the press box, chasing him around the stage before* **Martin** *falls into the ideas bin. A stunned silence, as* **Martin** *stares up at* **Jeremy**'s *manically smiling face.*

Jeremy   Right! That's the end of that scene! What's next?

Jeremy *goes backstage and comes back with* **Martin**'s *huge script. He opens it up and throws it at* **Martin**, *forcing him back into the bin.* **Martin** *looks through the script.*

Martin   The briefing room.

Jeremy   What's that?

---

[33] JS: I'm a fan of long and elongated fart noises, interrupted by shorter more staccato fart noises. Try to surprise both Martin and the audience.

Martin   It's a scene where the leader gets briefed.

Jeremy   Sounds amazing, let's go!

Jeremy *wheels* **Martin** *around in the bin and then tips him out onto the stage.*

Jeremy   Right, so this is my office, is it? Where's my chair?

Martin   We don't have a –

Jeremy   Well, find one!

Martin *runs to the dressing room and grabs a chair.* **Jeremy** *sits in it.*

Jeremy   And my foot stool?

Martin   Really?

Jeremy *forces* **Martin** *down into one knee,* **Jeremy** *puts his feet on him.*

Jeremy   Okay. Brief me.

Martin   The citizens are getting angry about gentrification. They are saying that there is no affordable housing and this is causing discontent amongst –

Jeremy   Woah, woah, woah . . . Make the briefing briefer.

Martin   Problem with affordable housing.

Jeremy   Briefer.

Martin   Problem.

Jeremy   Make it a sound?

Martin   Pfft.

Jeremy   Different sound?

Martin   AHHHHHH.

Jeremy   Turn it into a nursery rhyme!

Martin   What?

Jeremy   Turn it into a nursery rhyme, with Kevin on the keys. 1, 2, 3 . . .

Jeremy *gestures for music.* **Kevin** *plays 'Twinkle Twinkle Little Star' on the piano,* **Martin** *sings his lines to the tune.*

Martin   Problem with affordable housing. Lots of expensive places, no one can afford to live in. Working families, especially in the age bracket thirty-five to forty-five, are being pushed out to far away neighbourhoods. There is better coffee and more interesting food. But no one is actually . . . happy.

Jeremy   Hooray! Well done, Martin. That was great, what's next?

Martin   The French ambassador enters.

Jeremy   Go on then. Bring him in then.

Martin   Really?

Martin *spins around and becomes the French ambassador.* **Jeremy** *starts putting fists up to him, shadow boxing him and throwing plastic babies at him.*

Martin   Bonjour! Je m'appelle L'ambassadeur? (**Jeremy** *begins to box at* **Martin**.) Woah, où est la piscine? Je m'appelle Martin!

Jeremy   Right, we're done with that scene. What's next, give me that.

Jeremy *grabs the script and places it on the chair centre stage. As he goes through it he is ripping out the boring pages. The atmosphere is changing, a creeping sense of dread.*[34]

Martin   Be careful with that please –

Jeremy   What else is there? 'Tobias wows the UN convention.' Boring. Should have been cut anyway.

---

[34] R+C: This is the beginning of Jeremy's full descent from playful populist to maniacal dictator. We reflected this with the soundscore building a sense of impending doom.

Martin   Jeremy, please, there's only one copy.

Jeremy   Tobias solves the country's economic woes? What does that even mean?!

Martin   This is all my work –

Jeremy   What does this say? Oh yes, I remember this. (*Reading from the script.*) 'Tobias sees a group of angry rioters intent on destruction. Tobias: Friends, I understand your pain. Let's go and discuss this rationally and we will find a way together. The rioters immediately relax and hug each other . . .' Martin, this is ridiculous!

Martin   You've never said any of this before, Jeremy!

Jeremy   Who is this Tobias guy? He's an absolute joke.

Jeremy *is ripping more and more pages out. He eventually rips up the whole script, pages are flying all around them.* **Martin** *ends up scrambling on the floor for the pages.*

Martin   Tobias is a carefully considered and thought-out character –

Jeremy   Blah, blah, blah. Everything he says makes no sense! I've never understood what he's saying, (*Gesturing to the audience.*) I don't think they do either.

Martin   That's a matter of opinion. He's smart and clever and he thinks about the issues –

Jeremy   I've got it!

The soundscape of impending doom is growing and becoming more apparent.

Martin   What?

Jeremy   This play doesn't solve the problems because Tobias isn't a real leader. He just talks and talks and talks but he doesn't do anything. That's why it's so fucking long! You need someone with a bit of grit who gets stuff done, a real action man, do you know what I mean?

Martin   Not really.

Jeremy   They need to be tough, strong, someone that people will believe in. Where do I start?

Martin   Jeremy, where is this going?

Jeremy   I need an image. That's a good place to start. I need to look like someone people want to follow. I need a portrait!

Martin   A portrait?

Jeremy   This is ridiculous. Every leader has their own portrait, don't they?

Martin   I'm not sure what you want me to do?

Jeremy   Draw me.

Martin   I can't draw.

Jeremy   Well find me someone who can, an artist!

Martin   You want me to call –

Jeremy   No, look out there. (*Gesturing towards the audience.*) There must be an artist here somewhere. Pick someone who looks like an artist.

Jeremy *digs into his ideas big and reveals a huge drawing pad and a pen and gives it to* **Martin** *who scuttles into the audience to find someone who 'looks like an artist'.*[35]

Martin (*to audience member*)   What's your name? Would you mind being our artist?

Jeremy   Right, (*name of audience member*) you're gonna do my portrait, OK? I'm thinking of going subtle, just me in the chair. I need you to capture my authority, my charisma . . . Also make me look macho, that's very important. Kevin could you play something cultural? (**Kevin** *starts to play a tune on the piano.*) No, you know what, this is isn't right. Kevin! Go back to the playlist. Track ten.

---

[35] R+C: Here the house lights go up onto the audience and stay up on them until their involvement in the first half comes to an idea. It's an important signifier as their complicity in the next ten minutes is essential to the show working.

'Ride of the Valkyries' bursts from the speakers, **Jeremy** *screams in delight and tears his shirt off.*

Jeremy   Yes! This is way more manly. (*To the audience member artist.*) How is it looking? Hmmm, something's missing, isn't it. Martin, get over here.

Martin   Why?

Jeremy   I need your help. I need to look more powerful. I need to look like a world destroyer. Be a severed head! (**Jeremy** *gets* **Martin**'s *in a rough headlock.*) Yes, this is better, more to the point. I've got it, something better! Something heroic! Martin, be a horse!

Martin   I don't want to.

Jeremy   I don't care. Martin, be a fucking horse!

Martin   Can we stop this now?

Jeremy *grabs* **Martin**'s *tie and puts it in his mouth and stands on the chair to the side of* **Martin** *pretending to ride a horse.*

Martin   This is abuse, you need to get off me –

Jeremy   That's it. Maybe draw a mountain behind me and the horse? Maybe we have reached the top of the mountain?[36] Yes, that's the one. How is it? Show me. (*The audience member shows the rest of the audience the portrait.*) Wow. That is amazing. You're really good.[37] Martin, get it for me. Martin, hold that. Portrait there. Bit higher? Wow, looks great. (*To audience.*) Do you like it? Do you like me? I want to try something, when I stand on these steps I want to hear my adoring fan's adoration. (**Jeremy** *stands on steps in the auditorium and raises his arms, prompting adoration from the audience.*) More! Give me more adoration! And again![38]

---

[36] R+C: For inspiration have a Google of 'Putin topless on horse'.

[37] R+C: This bit most succeeds when the actor playing Jeremy finds lots of detail in reacting to what the artist has actually done. It's always funnier when Jeremy is effusively positive about the portrait, no matter how bad it is.

[38] R+C: It's really important that Jeremy has won the audience by this point and is riding the wave of their affection and enthusiasm. They need to have become willing accomplices.

(**Jeremy** *runs and jumps onto the chair in the centre of the stage.*)
Right everyone, stand up! Come on! Now I want everyone to
put their hand on your heart and repeat after me . . . I
believe in Jeremy! (**Jeremy** *points his microphone out to the
audience to get their response each time.*) Jeremy is the future!
Everything I do, I do it for Jeremy! Okay. That was great . . .
from some of you. But some of you aren't getting on board,
and I find that really disturbing. Some of you haven't even
got your hands on your chests[39] . . . If you're sitting next to
someone who isn't getting on board, put your hand up . . .[40]
I can wait all night. This is the show now. Because you see,
this doesn't work unless we're all on board.[41] If you've got a
problem with me, or what's going on here, why don't you
come up here and say it to my face. Come on!

Through all this **Martin** *has been looking on in horror. Eventually
he speaks out at* **Jeremy***'s suggestion on someone getting on stage.*

Martin   Jeremy, this is too much now, you have to stop!

Jeremy *and the action freezes. Music stops.*

Jeremy   What did you say?

Martin   I just think . . . This is horrible. We have to stop now.

Jeremy   Who the fuck is this guy? Do you know who this
guy is?

Martin   Okay, very funny, Jeremy.

Jeremy   Who said it was funny? *You* are interrupting *my*
show.

Martin   I didn't know it would turn into this.

---

[39] JS: Really look out into the audience and try to look at the people who aren't getting
on board. If they throw their hands onto their chests after you tell them to you can call
them out for being 'a bit late!'

[40] R+C: Sometimes this happens immediately, sometimes it doesn't happen at all. If
someone is ratted out then Jeremy should ask them what their problem is. If no one
rats on anyone then Jeremy goes on with the text 'I can stay here all night . . .'

[41] R+C: This can be either said directly to the audience member that has been ratted
out as a way of ending the conflict, or if no one is ratted out it can be said to the group.

Beat of silence.

Jeremy   Okay. I see. Okay, Martin. I think we need a little chat then. Come here, have a seat.

Jeremy *steps off the chair and gestures for* **Martin** *to sit there.*

Martin   I'm fine where I am.

Jeremy   What does that mean? Are you scared of me?

Martin   No.

Jeremy   Then what's the problem? Have a seat.

Martin *goes to sit and* **Jeremy** *pulls the chair from under him,* **Martin** *falls to the floor.* **Jeremy** *intensely grabs him while speaking into* **Martin***'s face.*

Jeremy   I just need you to go with it.

Martin   I don't feel comfortable with that.

Jeremy   Why? Because you're not leading it?

Martin   No.

Jeremy   Just come out with it, Martin! Stop hiding what you really feel. Let's have it out, man to man.

Martin   This isn't you, Jeremy.

Jeremy   There we go again, telling *me* who *I* am.

Martin   I want to leave.

Jeremy   Well, you can't, Martin. What's this?

Martin   It's my script.[42]

Jeremy   You don't need this. (**Jeremy** *throws the script across the stage.*) You're in my show now and I won't let you leave. It's time you realised that your show is a thing of the past.

---

[42] R+C: Martin has collected a lot of the thrown pages from the floor and put them back into a binder. Jeremy has become so crazed and power hungry, much of the last thirty minutes have flown from his mind.

It's dead. A fragment of history. This is the future and I need you to come on board.

Martin   What if I don't want to?

Jeremy   Great question. I'll tell you what happens to people who don't want to. It's simple.

Jeremy *reveals a gun and points the gun at* **Martin***'s head.* **Martin** *screams and puts himself in the brace position.* **Jeremy** *pulls the trigger and a bang sign comes out.*[43] **Jeremy** *laughs.*

Jeremy   Martin! It's a joke. Bang. We are having fun. This is a fun show now.[44]

After a few seconds of **Jeremy** *staring out to the audience holding his 'bang' gun,* **Martin** *cowering on the floor and* **Kevin** *poised at the piano, a silver curtain suddenly drops to the floor in front of the actors. It is a translucent curtain, and the audience can still see the performers behind it.*

End of Act One

(This is not an interval but goes into transition state before leading into Act Two.)

---

[43] JS: Just go to your local joke shop, get a 'bang' gun and spray paint it black. Job's a good 'un.

[44] R+C: Jeremy devilishly shares this with the audience, silently acknowledging the journey they've been on and their complicity from 'fun' balloons to the dark place they're now in.

The Transition. Part 1

After the moment between **Jeremy** *and* **Martin** *is held for a couple of seconds behind the silver curtain, the actors break the tension. They are no longer playing* **Jeremy** *and* **Martin**, *but rather are now the performers who were playing them. Although the audience can see them through the translucent curtain, the performers cannot see them and are in a private moment. They check in with each other, as one does after a show. Although we never hear their names, for the purpose of this text we will refer to the actors who originated the roles,* **Julian** *(who played* **Jeremy***),* **Matt** *(who played* **Martin***), and* **Khaled** *(who played* **Kevin***).*[45]

Julian   You alright?

Matt   Yeah . . .

Matt *gets off the floor and dusts himself off. Both* **Julian** *and* **Matt** *turn to* **Khaled** *who gives them a thumbs up to indicate 'good show'.* **Matt** *and* **Julian** *turn back to face each other, they hug. An explosive sound effect triggers the transition into Act Two.*

---

[45] R+C: When performing this moment, it is important that the actors return to the most underplayed 'real' versions of themselves. All the characterisation from Act One must drop to reveal the humans behind the clowning. These are the humans that we will need to connect with in Act Two. From this point we will be referring to the performers by their real names, although these are never revealed or spoken in the piece.

The Transition. Part 2

At the explosive sound effect, **Julian** *and* **Matt** *recoil from each other and spin upstage. They pull the curtain apart revealing a backstage area of lined mirrors framed by lightbulbs. They frantically clear the stage space of all the props from Act One, piling them into the ideas box. They then strip their clothes off down to their underwear, add them to the box and exit the space.*[46] *The space goes dark for a few moments.*

---

[46] R+C: There is a practical requirement for the stage to be cleared for Act Two, however the intention behind the clearing cannot be practical. It must be driven by a desire to dispose of something illegal or banned. It should have the energy of people shredding incriminating documents or evidence.

Director's Note on Act Two

If Act One was the freest version of the show that we could make, then Act Two is its direct opposite. This time the technique of clowning functions not to free up the performer and audience, but to restrict them. Act One is set in the audience's here and now, and Act Two is set in a future authoritarian regime that Act Two occupies the same 'theatre space' as Act One but is functioning completely differently due to a shift in political climate. This shift is a direct result of the action of Act One. It's essential that the same performers from the first act are the ones to take part in the second act. They are the people we see behind the curtain at the end of Act One. This is never explicitly said to the audience through text or time signifiers, and is sometimes interpreted with ambiguity, what's important though is the state of performance realism that is found in the transition carries through to the backstage moments of Act Two.

The two performers are forced to perform a piece of art for the regime in Act Two. When developing this act, we wanted to both formally and thematically reflect some of the common tropes of art in authoritarian regimes. Formally, they are nearly always performed with near perfect precision, in unison. There is often a greater emphasis placed on technique than individual expression. Authoritarianism doesn't tend to encourage colouring outside of the lines. Thematically, authoritarian art is often nostalgic for a golden era or past that perhaps never existed. This then ties into an obsession with glorifying military exploits but focusing more on heroism than horror. If individuals are depicted, they are very often in highly conventional relationships, or normative family units. Tonally, there is often a sentimentality at the heart of authoritarian art. If emotion is expressed, it is uncomplicated and one tone. This is the base from which we devised the clown routines that the performers must perform, and a good base to draw from if you're staging the scenes yourself.

The aesthetic of this act should be in complete contrast to the first act. It should be clean and sharp. The modern clowning of the first act, no nose and modern dress, is replaced by the most iconic and archaic form of clowning; the Pierrot clown. All white, with head caps and red noses. There's something dehumanising about this costume, and essential in removing the identities of the performers.

Much of the tension of the second act stems from the straight jacket nature of these restrictive routines. They must be move for move perfect or they must repeat them until they are. Perhaps most importantly, they are done in complete silence. The second act is almost entirely in silence, save for some words hesitantly and secretly shared between the two performers. Everything is policed and watched, from movements, to speech, even to thought.

The performers have two 'choices'; perform the prescribed routines or go back to where they've come from. As we first see them with bags on their heads cowering on the stools, we can only assume this is not a desirable choice. This danger is represented by the off-stage exit stage left, unseen but imagined by the audience. The audience's role has also changed this half. Gone is the open and playful complicity of Act One, replaced with prescriptive clapping for the routines and voyeuristic listening to the backstage moments between the performers.

Julian (left) and Matt (right) at the beginning of Act Two. They've just removed their bags and seen each other. Photography: Cesare De Giglio.

Matt and Julian in their full Pierrot clown costume. Photography: Cesare De Giglio.

The two behind the translucent curtain. The tension builds between the two.
Photography: Cesare De Giglio.

The desperate fight at the finale of The Goodbye. Photography: Cesare De Giglio.

Act Two

The light slowly filters through the silver curtain. **Julian** *and* **Matt** *are revealed to be sitting on stools at either end of a long line of mirrors. They're both in white underwear with bags on their heads.* **Khaled** *is in his chair with a bag on his head. He's in a new suit and sat at his piano. We stay with this image for a few beats. The silver curtain slowly rises.*

Tannoy You can take them off now.[47]

Julian *and* **Matt** *slowly take off the bags whilst sitting on the stools. They take in the space around them. They turn and notice each other and are locked in shock at seeing each other. They can hardly believe it. They stand up slowly and shuffle towards each other, they reach out and touch fingertips as if to see if the other is real.*[48] **Julian** *gestures as if to speak,* **Khaled** *instinctively plays keys as if to say, 'watch out'.*

Tannoy Hello. You know what you're here to do. Remember what you were told. What you used to do, forget that. If you are going to be a clown, be an actual clown. You need to make it funny. You need to make it clear. You need to make it precise. And you cannot deviate from the script.

Three scripts fall from the sky into the centre stage. They stand frozen staring at them.

Tannoy Pick them up.

Julian *cautiously picks up the scripts. He inspects them and gives two to* **Matt**. **Matt** *inspects them and places one on* **Khaled**'s *piano.* **Khaled** *picks it up. They all read the scripts.*

Tannoy Right. You need to get ready.

---

[47] R+C: This voice needs to sound like someone who works for the regime. It shouldn't be The Leader, or anyone too powerful. Just someone doing grunt work for the regime.
[48] R+C: This should be played as if they haven't seen each other in years. Perhaps disbelief that the other is alive.

The dressing room lights switch on. They go to the dressing tables where they discover their costumes. **Khaled** *begins to play music from the score. They begin to put on their costumes in this order: vest, trousers, jacket, cap. They unclip the white makeup and slowly apply it to their faces. Once they finish, they catch each other in the eye. Whilst getting changed,* **Julian** *flicks through the script one last time and keeps turning to face the front.* **Matt** *doesn't look at his script and remains faced towards the mirror. Once they both have everything on except their noses . . .*

Tannoy   The show is about to begin.

They turn to each other, put on their noses and turn to face the audience. They are Pierrot clowns. As the silver curtain opens . . .

Show Voice   Please welcome your entertainment.[49]

A drum roll from **Khaled**. **Matt** *and* **Julian** *slowly move out to the front of the stage. As the drum cymbal hits, two spotlights highlight the two clowns in a rigid, arms stretched expression of 'We're here!' After a bit too long,* **Khaled**'s *music starts, and they jump into the first routine. They walk forward and around the outer edge of the stage.*

Show Voice   The Reunion.

They stop, double take. Look at each other. They wave at each other. They go towards each other to shake hands but miss and end up on different sides. They try again but miss handshakes.

They see each other. Second missed handshake.

They see each other again. Limber up. Go in for the third handshake but lock arms and spin around to **Julian** *is facing away from* **Matt** *and they're both shaking the air.* **Matt** *spins* **Julian** *around but* **Julian** *slaps* **Matt** *on the head.* **Matt** *is dazed and drowsily moving about the space,* **Julian** *is trying to grab his hand to shake it like*

---

[49] R+C: The voice of the Show Voice must be the same as the voice at the top of Act One that tells the audience to turn off their phones. It's an important piece of storytelling that the audience are in the same space but in an altered environment, a change has taken place.

someone trying to grab hold of a bar of soap. They finally find each other's hands and shake hands.

The sign indicates for the audience to applause. The clowns take in the applause with stilted smiles and deferential nods.

Show Voice   The Soldier and the Boy.

The clowns leap into another silent mime duet. **Julian** *appears as a small boy, skipping into the space. He sees* **Matt** *entering the space, he's a soldier hunting with a gun.*

He shoots into the air punctuated by a cymbal from **Khaled**.

Julian's *legs are shaking. He fears the soldier.* **Matt** *sees* **Julian** *and winks at the audience.* **Matt** *blows up a mime balloon and hands it to* **Julian**. **Julian** *takes the balloon but then floats up into the air.* **Julian** *is floating in the sky, panicking.* **Matt** *shoots the balloon and* **Julian** *falls back to the ground.* **Julian** *gets up, dusts himself. They laugh.*

Matt *goes to leave but* **Julian** *calls after him and gestures for the gun.* **Matt** *gives* **Julian** *the gun and he stumbles under the weight.* **Matt** *points to a bird in the sky and* **Julian** *shoots it out of the air with a cymbal sound.* **Julian** *stumbles back and* **Matt** *walks forward to pick up the bird.* **Matt** *gives* **Julian** *the bird and takes the gun off him.*

As **Matt** *goes to leave,* **Julian** *calls out to him again and asks for the gun. They swap the gun and the bird.*

They both grow older. **Julian** *is now a soldier in a military parade and* **Matt** *is an old veteran attending. They recognise each other, do a double take.* **Matt** *mimes the bird that he shot many decades before,* **Julian** *points to the very same gun that he's still carrying.*

They smile at each other and **Julian** *pins a medal on* **Matt**. **Matt** *mimes a tear running down his cheek. They look out.* **Khaled** *creates a cymbal crash. The curtain falls just in front of them. The sign indicates for the audience to applause.*

End of Routine[50]

The two clowns can be seen through the silver curtain. They are back stage again but we can see them. They drop out of their performance mode. Both are clearly pumping with anxiety and adrenaline, **Matt** *more so who is staring rigidly out into the middle distance.* **Julian** *goes back to the mirror to flip through the script.* **Matt** *stays staring at the closed curtain and then slowly goes back to his chair. At some point they both take off their noses.*

When **Matt** *sits in his chair the soundscape begins.* **Matt** *is in shock, heavily breathing.* **Julian** *is busily going through the script.*[51]

Matt *slowly walks over to* **Julian***'s end of the mirrors.* **Julian** *is growing tense as he senses* **Matt** *approach. When* **Matt** *gets to* **Julian** *he touches him and* **Julian** *jumps.* **Matt** *crouches to* **Julian***'s ear.*

Matt (*whispers*)   I can't do this.

Julian *blurts out panicked laughter and attempts to brush it off by patting* **Matt** *on the shoulder.* **Matt** *is getting frustrated, he tries to repeat himself.*

Matt (*whispers*)   I can't /

Julian (*angrily*)   / Shh!

Matt *recoils from* **Julian***, who is seated, staring at* **Matt** *in the mirror.* **Matt** *is looking at the exit, just beyond* **Julian***. The exit glows.* **Julian** *clocks what* **Matt** *is looking at, and slowly gets up.* **Matt** *makes a rush to leave.* **Julian** *grabs him. They hold a moment of tension between them.* **Julian** *is frantically shaking his head.*

Tannoy   Are you ready to go back on?

---

[50] R+C: At this point the curtain coming down at the end of the routines denotes a change in space. When the curtain is raised they are exposed and are performing for the audience. With the curtain down, behind it the clowns are in the 'private' dressing room area. By 'private' the curtain is translucent so we can still see them, albeit partly blurred. We can also hear them through the built in microphones in the desk. If one is staging this without a translucent curtain, it's important to find a way to delineate between the public and private space.

[51] R+C: All of the sounds should be picked up by the microphones hidden in the dressing room tables. Even the smallest action and the slightest sound is amplified, adding to the voyeuristic quality of the backstage scenes.

They look at each other.

Julian   Yes!

Julian *desperately looks to* **Matt***, shakes his shoulders before* **Matt** *reluctantly relents.*

Matt   Yes.

They put on their noses. **Julian** *looks nervously at* **Matt** *before the silver curtain lifts.*

Show Voice   Please welcome back your clowns.

Drum roll and cymbal. On the cymbal they land in their 'We're here!' position.

Show Voice   The Shadow.

Khaled *begins a piano number to signal the start of the routine The Shadow,* **Julian** *and* **Matt** *jump into position, one behind the other. They jump back and start marching on the count, left foot first.* **Julian** *is following* **Matt** *exactly in step.*

Matt *stops and looks around, but 'can't see'* **Julian***.*

Julian *makes a shushing gesture to the audience.*

They shrug and continue marching along.

Matt *freezes.* **Julian** *taps him subtly, clearly not part of the routine.* **Matt** *is not smiling. He sends his hand back and then his foot.* **Julian** *mirrors him to stay out of sight.* **Matt** *swivels his foot back to try and catch* **Julian***.*

Julian *pokes his head around the other side of* **Matt** *and makes a shushing gesture.* **Matt** *shrugs and walks around and ends up in centre stage,* **Julian** *behind him.*

Matt *places his hands on his hips.*

Julian *pokes his arm through and strokes* **Matt***'s chin.*

Matt *clicks his fingers and* **Matt** *realises he has three hands.*

Julian *removes his hand.*

Matt *scratches his head,* **Julian** *puts his hands on* **Matt***'s hips.*

Matt *puts his hands on his own hips,* **Julian** *scratches* **Matt***'s head.*

Matt *is confused.*

Julian *puts his hand through* **Matt***'s arms and gestures 'a ha'.*

Matt *cottons on and gestures 'a ha'.*

Julian *pulls his arm away and* **Matt** *grabs his own arm and pulls himself around.*

Julian *ends up in front of* **Matt***. Confused, they shrug.*

Julian *leaps back to start walking again but* **Matt** *is frozen. It is now too much for him. He's overwhelmed.* **Julian** *looks back at him worried. Frozen in terror.*

Beep noise. Giant red light flashes.

The three look up in confusion. What do they do? Then we suddenly hear . . .

Show Voice   The Shadow.

The three look at each other confusedly, **Khaled** *jumps back on the keys,* **Julian** *clocks quicker than* **Matt** *that they need to do the routine again.*

He grabs **Matt** *and puts him in position.*

They jump back and start marching on the count, left foot first.

Julian *is following* **Matt** *exactly in step.*

Matt *stops and looks around, missing* **Julian***.*

Julian *makes a shushing gesture at the audience.*

He sends his hand back and then his foot. **Julian** *mirrors him to stay out of sight.*

Matt *swivels his foot back to try and catch* **Julian***.*

Julian *pokes his head around the other side of* **Matt** *and makes a shushing gesture.*

Matt *shrugs and walks around and ends up in centre stage,* **Julian** *behind him.*

Matt *places his hands on his hips.*

Julian *pokes his arm through and strokes* **Matt***'s chin.*

Matt *clicks his fingers and* **Matt** *realises he has three hands.*

Julian *removes his hand.*

Matt *scratches his head,* **Julian** *puts his hands on* **Matt***'s hips.*

Matt *puts his hands on his own hips,* **Julian** *scratches* **Matt***'s head.*

Matt *is confused.*

Julian *puts his hand through* **Matt***'s arms and gestures 'a ha'.* **Matt** *cottons on and goes 'a ha'.*

Julian *pulls his arm away and* **Matt** *grabs his own arm and pulls himself around.*

Julian *stops and feels for* **Matt***'s hand behind him. He grabs his wrist and pulls* **Matt** *through.* **Matt** *is confused. They see each other and laugh. They have finished the routine. A sense of relief from* **Julian***. The sign indicates 'applause' for the audience.*

Show Voice   Life and Death.

The sign shows the title Life and Death.

Julian *and* **Matt** *get into position.*

They draw a mime frame of their house and enter the door. **Matt** *and* **Julian** *are husband and wife.* **Matt** *digs the soil and plants the seeds.* **Julian** *stirs a pot. They wave to each other.*

Matt *pours the grain he has picked into* **Julian***'s bowl.*

Matt *goes back to the field and* **Julian** *becomes pregnant. They swivel around and the baby is in* **Julian***'s arms. They kiss the baby.*

Matt *becomes the baby and grows into a young man as* **Julian** *becomes an old woman.*

Julian *looks at* **Matt** *with pride and continues to stir the pot,* **Matt** *as the son leaves to dig outside.* **Julian** *looks fainter and fainter, he begins to cough and stumbles.* **Matt** *rushes over to catch him.*

Julian *is dying in his arms. He has one last breath and dies.* **Julian** *slips through* **Matt**'s *arms and floats away like a little angel ghost.*

The music changes and Khaled plays a sentimental number of the piano as Julian floats into the sky.[52]

Matt *is not okay and looks out.* **Julian**, *the angel ghost, is concerned and tries to keep the scene going.*

Julian *tries to catch* **Matt**'s *eyes but he's frozen, staring out to the audience.*

Loud beep. Red light.

They instantly go back to the start. **Julian** *tries to shake* **Matt** *out of it.*

Show Voice   Life and Death.

Julian *begins to draw the frame of the house, but* **Matt** *is shaking his head.*

He looks to **Julian** *as if to say, 'I can't go on',* **Julian** *grabs his hand to try and get him in the scene but* **Matt** *shakes his head and removes his nose.*

Loud beep. Red light.

Matt *starts walking backwards.*

The silver curtain drops leaving **Matt** *behind it and* **Julian** *stranded on stage.*

Julian *doesn't know what to do. This moment holds. He smiles. Half waves at the audience. Shrugs.* **Julian** *begins to do a halfhearted dance when the Show Voice interrupts . . .*

---

[52] R+C: The audience may laugh at this point. There's often an interesting cognitive dissonance that emerges when the audience are laughing at the routines whilst also aware of the horror the performers are going through.

Show Voice   The show is experiencing some minor
technical problems, please remain in your seats, the show
will begin again shortly.

Julian *dives under the curtain. It becomes translucent for the
audience, so they can now see* **Julian** *backstage.* **Julian** *walks over
to* **Khaled**. *They share a look.* **Khaled** *solemnly shakes his head and
looks down.*

Julian *sees the stool on the floor with* **Matt**'s *clown cap and clown
nose.*

*He picks them up and walks to the mirrors and makes a gesture. He's
desperate.*

He begins to knock on the mirror. **Julian** *is on the verge of breaking
down. His face is at the mirror. He speaks into it. To the people
behind the mirror.*

Julian   Wh – what do you want me to do now?

*He looks around desperately. He looks to the off-stage exit. After
contemplating he then walks towards the exit.*

Tannoy   What are you doing?

Julian *freezes in fear.*

Tannoy   No one told you that it was over.

Julian *glares at the tannoy*

Tannoy   Just sit and wait and you will be told what to do.

Julian *sits down, he's physically frozen in fear.*

There's a very loud static noise. **Julian** *grasps his hands over his
ears. Another loud static noise.*

Over the tannoy we hear **Matt**'s *voice.*

Matt (*on tannoy*)   Sorry. Sorry. I made a mistake.

Julian *reacts with a start. He looks towards the tannoy.*

Another long loud static noise.

Matt (*on tannoy*)   I won't do it again.

Long static noise.

Matt (*on tannoy*)   Him? Yes.

Julian *jumps up. He knows* **Matt** *is talking about him.*

Short static noise.

Matt (*on Tannoy*)   I can tell you things about him. He . . .

Long static noise. **Julian** *stands on a stool to try and hear. He is paranoid and scared.*

Matt (*on tannoy*)   He's . . . He's a traitor.[53]

Julian *is paralysed by fear. He is left standing on the stool.*

A tense pause.
Suddenly **Matt** *is pushed into the room.*
He flies across the floor and lands in a heap. He has a bag on his head.
Julian *jumps down and circles* **Matt**. **Matt** *is bracing himself, suggesting that he thinks he's about to be shot.*

Tannoy   You can take it off now.

Matt *takes the bag off his head. After a few moments he sees* **Julian** *and jumps back.*

A feeling of mistrust between them is held.

Julian *holds his gaze and is shaking with anger. He throws* **Matt**'*s clown cap at him. It hits the mirror.*

Julian *runs towards the exit from where* **Matt** *has come from,* **Matt** *stops him and throws him into the centre of the space.*

Julian *runs towards him and they're locked in a fierce wrestle.*

They're interrupted by the tannoy.

Tannoy   Are you ready to go back on?

---

[53] R+C: Please feel free to change the gender pronoun based on the preference of the performer and company staging the work.

Julian *is still struggling to get past him to the exit.*

Matt   Yes!

Julian *struggles but then stares into* **Matt***'s eyes as he responds intensely.*

Julian   Yes.

Matt *is relieved and walks past him to his table.* **Julian** *follows him with his eyes.*

Matt *is getting ready, putting his cap on.*

Julian *fiercely shoves* **Matt***'s clown nose down onto the desk, and puts his mask and nose on.* **Matt** *gets to the curtain before* **Julian***, who follows and stands next to him.*

The curtain rises.

Show Voice   Please welcome back your clowns!

The clowns walk forward, no drums this time but they do their 'We're here!' pose. The sign reads: The Goodbye.

Show Voice   The Goodbye.

They step into the lights.

The routine starts. They each walk off in an opposite direction down stage. They stop and look at each other and then walk back to each other.

They share a look, do a hand gesture and then walk off in the opposite directions again.

They walk back to each other, one points one way and one the other way.

They realise they are going opposite directions and have to say goodbye.

They look at each other and the clowns mime crying.

They wave goodbye to each other and shake hands. They try to walk off but can't release their hands.

They come together and try to work it out. They change hands and try to leave but their hands still won't release.

They twist and turn, going under each other's arms. Hands release.

They are free from each but are now standing in the wrong places, on the opposite side to the one they started on.

They then say goodbye and walk off in the wrong directions.

They realise their mistake and laugh at each other.

They walk back to each other, one points one way and one the other way. **Matt** *waves and walks.* **Julian** *pulls him back violently.*[54]

Julian *waves and walks.* **Matt** *pulls him back violently.* **Julian** *shoves* **Matt***.*

Matt *waves and walks.* **Julian** *pulls him back violently.* **Matt** *shoves* **Julian***.*

Julian *waves and walks.* **Matt** *grabs his leg and pulls him back.* **Julian** *slaps* **Matt***.*

Matt *spins off balance.* **Julian** *catches his leg and drops* **Matt** *to the floor.*

Matt *gets up from the floor.* **Julian** *is waiting for him. They circle each other.*

Julian *dives towards* **Matt***. They are grappling each other. It's a horrible struggle between them.*

Julian *manages to get* **Matt** *into a headlock and starts forcing him down onto the floor.*

The soundscape rises.

Julian *is strangling* **Matt***, and suddenly looks into his eyes. They pause still, horrified at what they're doing.*

They see each other for the first time and suddenly release.

---

[54] R+C: This needs to be the first physical act of violence in this scene that builds from simmering tension between the two. It can start as almost being part of the routine and then descends into a violent scrap.

Horrified, **Julian** *moves away from* **Matt,** *shaking with horror.*
Matt *slowly comes to* **Julian** *who allows him to touch him. They slowly dissolve physically into each other. They end up in a desperate hug. Breathing and heaving into each other.*

They look out at the audience. Fearful of who is watching them. They are gripping each other and slowly stand together.

Tannoy   Why have you stopped? You have to carry on.

Matt *and* **Julian** *are clinging onto each other. They look at* **Khaled.** *Then they look at the audience.*

Tannoy   Don't just stand there, get back into it.

They cling to each other in defiance. **Khaled** *understands this gesture and moves towards the drum.*

Tannoy   This is very dangerous what you are doing, do you understand?

Khaled *bangs the drum hard.* **Julian** *and* **Matt** *react in shock and look at him. He bangs again. He starts a drum beat and moves towards the centre stage.*

Tannoy   What're they doing? They can't do this, it's not allowed! They have to get back into their corner.

Khaled *continues the drumbeat.*

Tannoy   Just stop and think about what you are doing.

Khaled *continues the drumming and moves into the centre of the stage.* **Julian** *and* **Matt** *shuffle behind* **Khaled** *and put their hands on his shoulders.* **Khaled**'*s drumming becomes more fierce.*

Tannoy   Shit, shit, shit. Okay, what do we do? What do we –

Loud sirens start to blare.

Show Voice   Please evacuate the building. (*Repeats.*)

Julian *and* **Matt** *break away from* **Khaled.**

They realise they need to join the rebellion, **Julian** *tears his top off and runs to the mirrors and takes the white makeup and begins writing large crosses across the mirrors.*

Matt *runs towards the cymbal and takes a stick and starts smashing it.*[55]

Khaled *is playing the drum louder and louder, the sirens are beginning to crack.*

The sequence reaches a crescendo. The siren fades, the Show Voice slows and creaks to a stop.

Suddenly everything falls silent apart from **Khaled** *who is standing centre, still drumming.*

Julian *and* **Matt***, exhausted, stare at* **Khaled***. The last bastion of resistance.*

Khaled *slowly builds the drumbeat increasing in speed and volume as he slowly turns to face the audience.*

He builds to a final drumbeat as he raises his arm in the air. His arm stays aloft.

Blackout.

We don't hear the last drumbeat.

End.

---

[55] R+C: this needs to feel like a final act of defiance. They know they are going down, the consequences will not be good, but they are going down fighting and with resistance.